Little Pebble

What Are Blizzards?

by Mari Schuh

PEBBLE
a capstone imprint

Little Pebble is published by Pebble
1710 Roe Crest Drive,
North Mankato, Minnesota 56003
www.capstonepub.com

Library of Congress Cataloging-in-Publication Data
Names: Schuh, Mari C., 1975–author.
Title: What are blizzards? / by Mari Schuh.
Description: North Mankato, Minnesota : Pebble, a Capstone imprint, [2019] | Series: Little pebble. Wicked weather | Audience: Ages 4–8.
Identifiers: LCCN 2018029833 (print) | LCCN 2018031582 (ebook) | ISBN 9781977103369 (eBook PDF) | ISBN 9781977103291 (hardcover) | ISBN 9781977105462 (paperback)
Subjects: LCSH: Blizzards—Juvenile literature. | Snow—Juvenile literature.
Classification: LCC QC926.37 (ebook) | LCC QC926.37 .S38 2019 (print) | DDC 551.55/5—dc23
LC record available at https://lccn.loc.gov/2018029833

Editorial Credits
Nikki Potts, editor; Kyle Grenz, designer;
Heather Mauldin, media researcher; Tori Abraham, production specialist

Photo Credits
iStockphoto: DenisTangneyJr, 13, Miha9000, 19, Reptile8488, 15; Shutterstock: Alexey Lesik, 5, Danilovski, 21, Dmitriy Kochergin, 11, eddtoro, 17, Marc Bruxelle, 9, Tainar, cover, V J Matthew, 1, Yuliya Evstratenko,7

Printed in the United States PO007052

Table of Contents

What Is a Blizzard?

Lots of snow falls.

A strong wind blows.

A bad winter storm is here.

It is a blizzard!

Blizzards can happen when warm air rises over cold air. Snow forms.

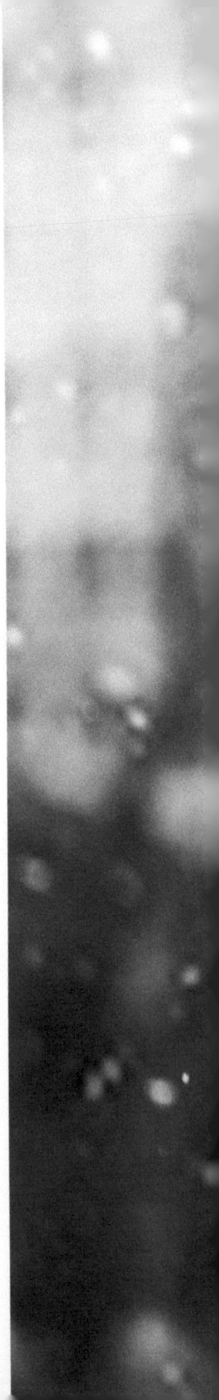

More and more snow falls.
It lasts for three hours or more.
Some blizzards last for days.

Whoosh!

Wind blows the snow.

It is hard to see.

Look!

Snow piles up.

The wind makes big drifts.

Beacon Hill
Resident
Permit
Parking
Only
drift

Staying Safe

Brr!

It is very cold.

It is best to stay inside.

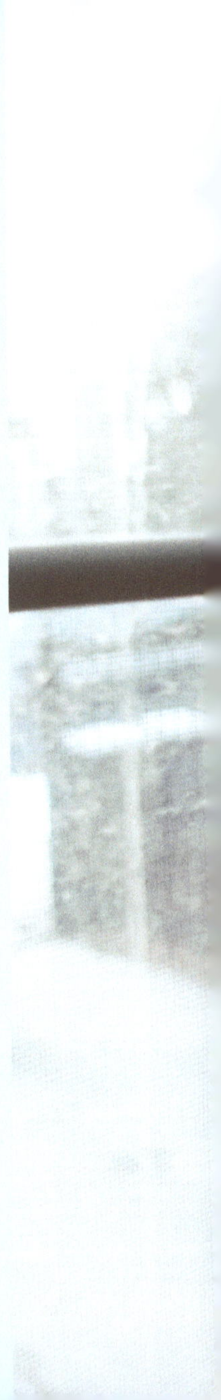

Temperatures can be

below zero.

People can get frostbite.

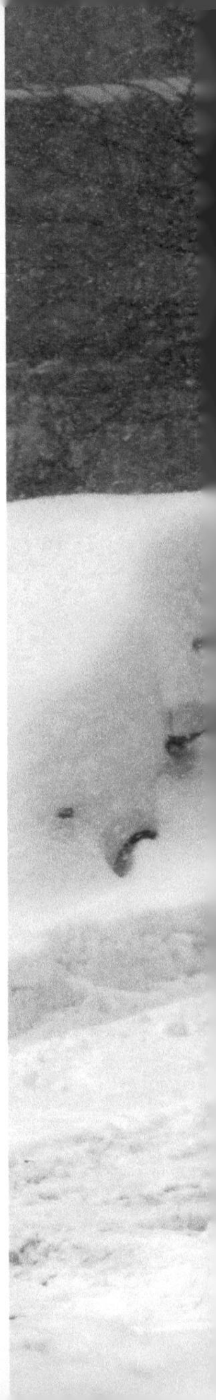

See the icy roads.

Cars slide on the ice.

They can crash.

People should not travel.

The blizzard is over.
The wind and snow
have stopped.
People dig out their cars!

Glossary

blizzard—a heavy snowstorm with strong wind

drift—a pile of snow made by strong wind

frostbite—a condition that happens when cold temperatures freeze skin

storm—bad weather; hurricanes, tornadoes, and blizzards are types of storms

temperature—the measure of how hot or cold something is

Read More

Jensen, Belinda. *A Snowstorm Shows Off: Blizzards.* Bel the Weather Girl. Minneapolis: Millbrook Press, 2016.

Raum, Elizabeth. *Blizzard!* Natural Disasters. Mankato, Minn.: Amicus Ink, 2017.

Schuetz, Kristin. *Severe Weather.* Understanding Weather. Minneapolis: Bellwether Media, 2016.

Internet Sites

Use FactHound to find Internet sites related to this book.

Visit www.facthound.com

Just type in 9781977103291 and go.

Critical Thinking Questions

1. Why are blizzards dangerous?
2. Name one way people can stay safe during a blizzard.
3. Why is it hard to see during a blizzard?

Index